STRESS FREE CHRISTMAS AND NEW YEAR SEASON

Importance Of Financial Planning And Avoiding Holiday Debt

THERESA A. MEDLEY

CHRISTMAS IS A
TIME FOR LOVE AND
TOGETHERNESS, BUT
IT'S ALSO AN
OPPORTUNITY TO
SPEND WISELY AS
WE APPROACH THE
NEW YEAR.

TABLE OF CONTENTS

INTRODUCTION

The Christmas and New year season can be a costly time for some individuals. Between purchasing presents for friends and family, facilitating or going to occasion gatherings, and making a trip to see family, the expenses can rapidly add up. Without legitimate financial preparation, it's not difficult to overspend and wind up in the red come the new year.

One method for keeping away from this is by setting a financial plan for your vacation spending. Deciding the amount you can bear to spend on gifts, enhancements, and different costs, you can try not to overspend and remain inside your means. Making a financial plan can assist you with focusing on your spending and spotlight on what means quite a bit to you during special times of year.

One more significant part of financial preparation during the Christmas and new year season is setting aside cash consistently. By saving a modest quantity of cash every month, you can develop an occasion reserve that will assist with covering your costs when the opportunity arrives. This can assist with mitigating the financial pressure that frequently goes with special times of year, permitting you to partake in the season without stressing over cash completely.

As well as planning and saving, it's additionally essential to be aware of your ways of managing money during special times of year. With such countless enticing deals and advancements, it's not difficult to become involved with the fervor of shopping and overspend. By being aware of your buys and adhering to your spending plan, you can keep away from superfluous costs and guarantee that you're not placing yourself in a troublesome financial circumstance.

At long last, searching out financial guidance and assets can be unbelievably useful during the Christmas season. Whether it's talking with a financial consultant, understanding books or articles on financial preparation, or using planning applications, there are many devices accessible to assist you with dealing with your funds during special times of year. By exploiting these assets, you can acquire important experiences and direction that will assist you with making informed choices about your cash.

Generally, financial preparation during the Christmas and new year season is fundamental for keeping up with financial security and genuine serenity. By setting a financial plan, setting aside cash, being aware of your spending, and searching out financial counsel, you can guarantee that you're ready to completely partake in the Christmas and new year season without stressing over cash. With the right way to deal with financial preparation, you can make enduring recollections with your friends and family and enter the new year with certainty and financial security.

In this book, we will discuss the significance of financial preparation during the Christmas season, feature the advantages it brings, and give viable exhortation to assist us with overcoming this difficult season with financial genuine serenity.

CHAPTER ONE

Importance Of Financial Planning During Christmas And New Year Season

The Christmas season can introduce special financial challenges as the pressure of purchasing presents, voyaging and going to festivities can prompt overspending and monetary pressure.

It is critical to comprehend these difficulties and track down proactive ways of dealing with your assets during this time.

One of the greatest financial challenges at Christmas is the strain to spend excessively. Given the pressure of purchasing presents for loved ones and going to relaxed works out, it's quite easy to examine the spending plan and aggregate commitments.

Coordinating your funds can assist you with making a reasonable monetary arrangement and spotlight on spending so you can partake in the season without undermining your monetary prosperity.

Another challenge is the amazing costs that frequently emerge at specific seasons. From late gifts to travel changes, these unexpected costs can rapidly add up and mess up your spending plan.

Incorporating a possibility hold in your financial understanding, you can be more ready to take care of these expenses without undermining your in general financial objectives.

What's more, the Christmas season can energize shopping, as the excitement during this time can twist the appraisal of expenditure.

A financial foundation can assist you with zeroing in on your necessities and stay away from superfluous buys. It guarantees that you adhere to your financial arrangement and make an effort not to assume pointless obligation.

At last, it is essential to consider the continuous effect of occasion spending.

Beginning the New Year with great financial game plans can assist you with keeping away from the strain of liabilities after a free arrangement and make an uplifting climate for your financial prosperity in the approaching year.

By zeroing in on your investment funds, recognizing open ways to reserve funds, and planning for surprising expenses, you can guarantee your assets are in excellent condition as the new year starts.

In general, understanding the financial challenges of special times of year and tracking down approaches to proactively deal with your assets can assist you with partaking in the merriments without endangering your financial prosperity. Integrating financial planning into the Christmas season, you can get ready to return in the new year and stay away from post-holiday debt.

Other financial challenges during the Christmas season incorporate the tensions of movement and family visits, which can prompt inflated costs for transportation, housing and food.

Preparing and setting a sensible travel financial plan can assist you with trying not to overspend around here.

Another challenge is the need to go to occasions and parties, which can bring about extra expenses for food, beverages and diversion. Defining limits and focusing on the occasions that are generally critical to you can assist you with dealing with these costs and stay away from financial pressure.

Furthermore, the Christmas season can raise a feeling of examination and contest while giving presents, which can make a craving to overspend to stay aware of others.

It's memorable's critical that the considerations and sentiments behind a present are a higher priority than the expense. Setting sensible assumptions with your friends and family can assist with alleviating this tension.

At long last, it very well may be challenging to deal with the effect of occasional deals and advancements, as the compulsion to exploit offers and limits can prompt superfluous spending. Adhering to a spending plan and keeping away from drive buys will keep you on target to accomplish your financial objectives.

Monitoring these financial challenges and integrating proactive methodologies into your excursion arranging will assist you with exploring the season with financial strength and genuine serenity.

Chapter Two

Understanding The Financial Challenges Of Christmas And New Year

The Christmas season, including Christmas and New Year, is a period of delight and festivity.

In any case, it can bring financial challenges for some people and families. Understanding these difficulties is pivotal for pursuing informed financial choices and keeping up with financial prosperity during this merry period.

In this book, we will discuss a few normal financial challenges that emerge during Christmas and New Year, alongside tips to conquer them.

Overspending:

One of the greatest monetary difficulties during this season is overspending. The strain to purchase presents, adornments, and enjoy occasion celebrations can prompt imprudent buys and surpassing your spending plan.

To handle this challenge, consider making a point by point financial plan that incorporates every single essential cost, focus on your spending, and oppose the impulse to overspend.

Increased Costs:

The Christmas season frequently accompanies extra costs, for example, travel costs, facilitating gatherings, and going to get-togethers.

These extra financial weights can overburden your financial plan. Prepare by assessing these expenses and changing your financial plan in like manner. Search for ways of saving, for example, carpooling for movement, facilitating potluck get-togethers, or setting spending limits on gifts.

Debt Collection:

Numerous people resort to charge cards or advances to cover their vacation costs, prompting expanded obligation. Amassing obligation during this time can have long haul outcomes on your financial dependability.

Keep away from inordinate getting and center around spending inside your means. Consider elective choices like hand crafted gifts, acts of kindness, or encounters that don't include huge expenses.

Emotional Spending:
The Christmas season frequently sets off feelings of affection, appreciation, and liberality.
Nonetheless, it is fundamental not to allow these feelings to cloud your financial judgment. Try not to make rash buys exclusively founded on feelings.
All things considered, plan your spending and settle on insightful choices. Keep in mind, the genuine soul of the time lies in making vital minutes with friends and family, not material possessions.

Post-Occasion financial Pressure:
The outcome of the Christmas and New year season can bring financial pressure as bills and costs begin to stack up.
To adapt to this challenge, focus on and deal with your costs astutely. Make a reimbursement plan for any obligations caused, cut back on pointless consumptions, and spotlight on modifying your reserve funds. Being proactive and sensible about

your funds will assist with lightening post-occasion stress.

Conclusion:

Understanding the financial challenges related with the Christmas and New Year season is the most important move towards dealing with your funds successfully. By making a spending plan, preparing, opposing emotional spending.

Increased Expenses And Financial Stress

During the Christmas and New Year season, there are a few factors that can add to expanded costs and financial pressure.

One of the primary contributors is the strain to travel and see family. Many individuals feel committed to make the excursion to see friends and family during special times of year, which can prompt tremendous costs for transportation, facilities, and feasts.

Flights and train tickets are in many cases more costly during this time, and lodging rates can likewise be higher because of expanded request. Also, feasting out and engaging relatives can add up rapidly, particularly assuming you are facilitating visitors in your home.

One more wellspring of Financial pressure during the Christmas season is the assumption to take part in get-togethers and social occasions.

Whether it's going to office parties, occasion meals with companions, or New Year's Eve festivities, these occasions frequently accompany extra expenses for food, beverages, and amusement. It tends to be trying to adjust the longing to partake in these celebrations with the need to adhere to a financial plan.

Gift-giving is a financial challenge during special times of year. There is many times strain to purchase presents for relatives, companions, and associates, and the expense of gifts can rapidly add up.

Many individuals feel a sense of urgency to spend beyond what they can manage the cost of to stay aware of others or to show their affection and appreciation through material things.

At last, the effect of occasional deals and advancements can add to financial pressure during the Christmas season. While it very well may be enticing to exploit arrangements and limits, this can prompt motivation buys and overspending.

The steady siege of commercials and advancements can make it challenging to adhere to a financial plan and stay away from superfluous buys.

In general, the blend of expanded costs for movement, get-togethers, present giving, and the bait of occasional deals can make huge financial pressure during the Christmas and New Year season. People must be aware of these challenges and to prepare to deal with their funds actually during this time.
Setting reasonable spending plans, focusing on spending, and being aware of the genuine importance of special times of year can assist with easing a portion of the monetary strain related with this season.

Different variables that might add to expanded spending and monetary pressure during the Christmas season include:

1. Home Decorations and Occasion Costs

Many individuals want to enhance their home for these special seasons, which can bring about extra costs for enrichments, lights, and other occasion things.

Furthermore, facilitating occasion social events or house gatherings can bring about higher service bills and food costs.

2. Travel Costs

Notwithstanding transport and convenience costs, there are in many cases other travel-related costs an extended get-away, for example, food or pet consideration, stopping expenses and baggage transport costs.

3. Magnanimous Gifts

Gifts to others are a significant piece of special times of year, however they can be a financial weight. Many individuals feel committed to give to good cause or partake in pledge drives, which can affect their financial plan.

4. Occasional Exercises and Entertainment

Going to shows, shows and other occasional occasions during special times of year can be a tremendous cost, particularly for families with children.

Additionally, partaking in winter sports or exercises, for example, skiing or ice skating can build your financial burden.

5. Expanded Energy Expenses

Colder climate during the Christmas season can prompt higher warming and electric bills, particularly assuming you are engaging visitors or utilizing extra lights and apparatuses during the celebrations.

6. Health And Wellbeing Costs

While appreciating occasion feasts and treats, certain individuals might bring about higher medical services expenses to really focus on their physical and psychological well-being during this time.

7. Vacation

People who get some much needed rest during special times of year might experience a deficiency of pay or be expected to take paid excursion, which could influence what is happening.

Individuals should think about these elements while arranging the Christmas season and arriving at informed conclusions about apportioning their assets to keep away from financial pressure.

Psychological And Emotional Impact Of Financial Burden

The psychological and emotional impact of financial strain during the Christmas season can be enormous.

The strain to live up to cultural assumptions and give your friends and family an extraordinary excursion experience can prompt pressure, uneasiness, and deficiency.

This can be particularly valid for individuals who are now battling monetarily or are living check to check.

Consistent stresses over cash and stressing over not having the option to manage the cost of gifts, trips, or other excursion costs can adversely affect your psychological wellness. This can prompt sensations of culpability, disgrace and dissatisfaction, as well as sensations of segregation and forlornness on the off chance that you can't go to festivities like others.

Financial pressure during special times of year can affect connections, as people might feel constrained to burn through cash they don't have or struggle with relatives over financial plan and spending choices.

Furthermore, the emotional cost of Financial pressure can stretch out past the Christmas season and lead to long haul pressure and uneasiness about cash the executives and future monetary steadiness.

For individuals encountering financial pressure while holiday, it is vital that their psychological and emotional prosperity starts things out.
Enrolling the help of friends and family, dealing with yourself, and looking for help from an expert when required will assist you with better dealing with the mental impacts of financial pressure.
Moreover, tracking down approaches to reevaluate special times of year as a period of association, appreciation, and significant encounters instead of a period of material belongings can assist with

lightening a portion of the profound strain that accompanies financial pressure.

The psychological and emotional effect of financial pressure during the Christmas season show itself in actual side effects, for example, migraines, stomach issues and rest problems.
Steady stresses over cash can prompt a decrease in generally speaking prosperity and deteriorate existing emotional well-being issues like sorrow and uneasiness.

For individuals with kids, the strain to give a magical occasion experience can be especially overpowering, prompting insecurities and culpability when they can't measure up to their youngsters' assumptions.
This can cause you to feel like a disappointment as a parent and lead to sensations of stress and uneasiness.

Correlation with others and apprehension about judgment from loved ones can prompt sensations of disgrace and uselessness, which greatly affect psychological wellness during the Christmas season.

Financial pressure during special times of year can prompt negative contemplations and self-analysis, as people might feel like they are not satisfying cultural norms or their own assumptions for these special seasons.

As well as looking for help from friends and family and dealing with yourself, tracking down ways of making new customs and encounters that don't include burning through cash can assist with facilitating a portion of the profound cost of financial pressure during special times of year mitigate.

This might incorporate chipping in, investing energy with friends and family, or tracking down euphoria in simple delights.

The psychological and emotional of financial burden during the Christmas season prompt sensations of separation and dejection.

As people might feel unfit to partake in friendly exercises or get-togethers because of monetary limitations, they might encounter a feeling of disengagement from their local area and friends and family.

Besides, the pressure of Financial strain can prompt stressed connections and clashes inside families and among companions. The strain to live up to assumptions and the powerlessness to do so can make pressure and hatred, prompting a breakdown in Communication and emotionally supportive networks.

The steady stress over cash and the powerlessness to accommodate friends and family can likewise prompt sensations of responsibility and disgrace. This can influence a singular's confidence and feeling of worth, prompting a pessimistic mental self view and a lessening in general mental prosperity.

Besides, the financial burden during the Christmas season influence a singular's capacity to partake in the merriments and experience happiness. The consistent distraction with cash and the failure to completely take part in occasion customs can prompt sensations of bitterness and disillusionment.

Generally speaking, the psychological and emotional effect of monetary burden during the Christmas season can be huge, influencing one's psychological well-being, connections, and by and large prosperity.

It is significant for people encountering financial strain to look for help, practice taking care of oneself, and track down elective ways of commending and find euphoria during the Christmas season.

CHAPTER THREE

Setting Financial Goals For A Stress Free Christmas And New Year

Setting out financial objectives for a tranquil Christmas and New Year's includes cautious preparation and planning.

Here are an itemized moves toward assist you with accomplishing this:

Assess Your Ongoing Financial Circumstance

Begin by assessing your ongoing pay, costs, and any remaining obligations. This will provide you with an unmistakable image of your monetary wellbeing and assist you with setting practical goals.

Determine Your Vacation Spending Limit

Settle on a particular sum that you can easily spend during the Christmas season without stressing your funds. Think about your pay, investment funds, and some other financial commitments you may have.

Make A Rundown And Focus On

Make a rundown of the relative multitude of costs you anticipate during the Christmas and New Year's time span.

This can incorporate gifts, designs, food, travel, and diversion. Focus on your costs in view of their significance and dispense reserves accordingly.

Create A Financial Plan

With your spending breaking point and cost list as a primary concern, make a definite spending plan. Partition your spending across various classifications and appoint explicit sums. Make certain to leave some space for surprising expenses.

Save Ahead Of Time

Assuming that your spending plan surpasses your ongoing financial limit, begin saving great ahead of time. You can save a specific measure of cash every month paving the way to the Christmas season to guarantee you have an adequate number of assets when the time comes.

Track Your Spending

All through the Christmas season, monitor your costs to guarantee you stay acceptable for you. Use applications or accounting sheets to screen your spending and make changes if necessary.

Seek Reasonable Other Options

Search for cash saving tips without settling for less on the occasion soul. Think about hand crafted gifts, Do-It-Yourself enrichments, or deciding on reasonable encounters rather than lavish outings.

It may be enticing to depend on Mastercards or advances to back your vacation costs. Notwithstanding, this can prompt financial pressure over the long haul. Adhere to your spending plan and try not to acquire except if totally necessary.

Explore Arrangements And Limits

Exploit occasional deals, limits, and coupons to extend your financial plan further. Analyze costs, shop in an intelligent way, and consider mass buys for things that won't perish.

Focus On Encounters And Significant Associations
Recall that the Christmas season is tied in with investing quality energy with friends and family, not simply material belongings. Focus on encounters and significant associations over extreme gifts.

Plan For The New Year
As you put forth financial objectives for a calm Christmas, remember to anticipate the New Year too. Consider setting goals connected with saving, obligation reimbursement, or moving along.

Here are some extra stress out objectives for a peaceful Christmas and New Year season
Focus On Taking Care Of Oneself
Try to plan normal taking care of oneself exercises like cleaning up, rehearsing care, or getting a back rub to unwind and re-energize.

Improve On Embellishments

Rather than going all out with intricate designs, decide on a less difficult methodology. Center around a couple of key regions or designs that give you pleasure, and try not to overpower yourself with unnecessary ornamentation.

Set A Spending Plan
Plan your vacation costs ahead of time and adhere to a spending plan to stay away from financial pressure. Consider natively constructed gifts or acts of kindness that don't need spending a great deal of money.

Practice Appreciation
Take time every day to ponder what you're thankful for. This can assist with moving your concentration from stress to appreciation, cultivating a more certain outlook during the occasion season.

Delegate Errands
Feel free to request help or representative undertakings to other people. Whether it's cooking, cleaning, or gift wrapping, sharing the responsibility

can reduce pressure and make a feeling of teamwork.

Plan Personal Time

Timetable customary times of rest and unwinding all through the Christmas season. Whether it's a calm night at home or an end of the week escape, try to re-energize and enjoy reprieves from the bustling festivities.

Embrace Flaw

Recall that special times of year don't need to be great. Permit yourself to relinquish unreasonable assumptions and embrace the defects that accompany the season.

Center around making significant recollections instead of taking a stab at perfection.

Practice Using Time Productively

Make a timetable or plan for the day to assist with dealing with your time really. Focus on errands, set reasonable cutoff times, and keep away from overcommitting yourself to keep away from superfluous stress.

Stay Dynamic

Integrate actual work into your everyday practice to lessen pressure and lift your temperament.

Whether it's taking a walk, rehearsing yoga, or participating in a colder time of year sport, remaining dynamic can assist you with overseeing pressure during the occasion season.

Connect With Friends And Family

Find opportunity to associate with your friends and family and focus on quality time together.

Whether it's getting sorted out a family game evening or facilitating a virtual get-together, encouraging significant associations can give pleasure and diminish pressure during the occasion season.

Remember, these objectives can be custom fitted to your own inclinations and conditions. Pick the ones that impact you and adjust them to make a tranquil Christmas and New Year season that suits your requirements.

Assessing Your Current Financial Solution

Apportioning resources for gifts, enhancements, and festivities requires wary planning and thought. The following are a couple of clues to help you with exploiting your budget.

Set a financial arrangement Conclude the sum you can tolerate spending on gifts, beautifications, and good times. Contemplate your overall financial situation and spotlight on your expenses.

Make A Gift List

Make an overview of people you really want to buy presents for and assign a specific aggregate for each person. This will help you with staying facilitated and promise you don't overspend.

Research Expenses And Contemplate Deals

Preceding making any purchases, research costs and dissect deals from different stores or online stages. Look for cutoff points, coupons, or remarkable progressions that can help you with setting aside cash.

Think About Hand Crafted Or Redid Gifts

Excellent or tweaked gifts can be a savvy and pragmatic decision. Ponder your capacities and gifts, and examine making something exceptional for your treasured ones.

Prepare For Beautifications

If possible, plan your upgrades well early. This will offer you a chance to take a gander at the best expenses and capitalize on any arrangements or cutoff points. Consider reusing plans from prior years or gaining them from colleagues and family.

Focus On Experiences Over Material Things

As opposed to focusing in solely on material gifts, consider giving experiences like passes to a show, a spa day, or a week's end escape.

These experiences can make getting through memories without overpowering your spending plan.

Keep Track Of Your Spending

All through the Christmas season, screen your spending to ensure you're sticking to your monetary arrangement.

Use arranging applications or fundamental bookkeeping sheets to screen your expenses and make changes if necessary.

Remember, the central thing is the spirit of the Christmas season, not how much money you spend. Base on huge movements, contributing energy with loved ones, and making an euphoric air.

Budgeting Strategies For A Joyful Christmas And New Year

The Christmas season is a period of satisfaction, love, and festivity. Be that as it may, it can bring financial pressure in the event that not oversaw as expected.

Carrying out successful planning methodologies, you can guarantee an upbeat and peaceful Christmas and New Year season.

In this book,we will talk about a few tips to help you plan carefully and capitalize on your vacation expenses.

Set a Practical Spending plan:

Begin by deciding the amount you can bear to spend during the Christmas season. Think about your pay, costs, and any extra investment funds you might have. Set a sensible spending plan that lines up with your monetary circumstance to stay away from overspending.

Make a Rundown :

Make a complete rundown of the relative multitude of costs you anticipate during the Christmas season. This might incorporate gifts, embellishments, travel costs, food, and diversion. Focus on your rundown in light of what makes the biggest difference to you and dispense reserves accordingly.

Take Potential benefit of Deals and Limits:
Watch out for deals, limits, and special proposals all through the Christmas season. Shop decisively by contrasting costs of various retailers prior to making any buys. Use coupons, online arrangements, and cashback potential chances to boost your savings.

Plan and Plan Dinners Ahead of time:
Food costs can rapidly accumulate during the Christmas season. Plan your dinners ahead of time and make a shopping rundown to keep away from drive purchasing. Exploit deals on durable things, and think about purchasing in mass for more ideal arrangements.

Moreover, facilitating potluck-style get-togethers can convey the expense and make a merry local area atmosphere.

Limit Diversion Use:
Rather than costly excursions and occasions, search out free or minimal expense occasion amusement choices. Go to local area occasions, nearby shows, or appreciate comfortable film evenings at home. Investigate outside exercises like ice skating, climbing, or visiting occasion light shows, which can give essential encounters without breaking the bank.

Utilize Innovation:
There are different planning applications and devices accessible that can help you in following your costs and adhering to your spending plan. Utilize these assets to screen your spending, recognize areas of progress, and change your financial plan accordingly.

CHAPTER FOUR

Creating A Comprehensive Christmas And New Year Budget

Making a thorough Christmas and New Year financial plan is an incredible method for guaranteeing that you can partake in the Christmas season without overspending or straying into the red.

Through cautiously arranging and following your costs, you can deal with your funds successfully despite everything having an important and charming Christmas season.

Bit by bit guide on the most proficient method to make a thorough Christmas and New Year budget:

Determine Your General Financial Plan:
Begin by concluding how much cash you can bear to distribute towards your vacation costs. Think about your pay, investment funds, and some other monetary commitments you have. Be reasonable about what you can manage and stay away from the compulsion to overspend.

Make A Rundown, Everything Being Equal:

Record every one of the potential costs you anticipate during the Christmas season. This might incorporate gifts, embellishments, food and beverages, travel costs, beneficent gifts, parties, and some other exercises or customs you typically partake in.

Remember to incorporate any extra costs like wrapping paper, cards, or postage.

Allocate Assets To Each Expense Classification:

Subsequent to posting every one of your costs, allot assets to every class in view of their need and significance. Consider what makes the biggest difference to you and your friends and family and relegate a sensible sum to every classification. Be careful not to overspend in any one region and leave space for surprising costs.

Set Spending Limits For Gifts: Gift-giving is a tremendous cost during the Christmas season. Set a spending limit for each individual or for the general gift financial plan. This will assist you with remaining inside your means and keep away from inordinate spending.

Think about options in contrast to costly gifts, like high quality things, encounters, or smart gestures.

Research And Look At Costs:

Prior to making any buys, research costs and analyze them across various stores or online stages. Exploit deals, limits, and coupons to get the best arrangements.

Cost correlation sites and applications can be useful devices in tracking down the best costs for explicit items.

Track your costs:

Consistently screen and track your costs all through the Christmas season. Keep receipts and record each buy to guarantee it stays acceptable for you.

This should be possible utilizing a bookkeeping sheet, planning application, or even pen and paper. Consistently exploring your spending will assist you with remaining responsible and make any fundamental adjustments.

Consider Elective Festivals:

On the off chance that your financial plan is tight, ponder elective ways of praising special times of year without overspending. This could incorporate facilitating a potluck supper with loved ones, coordinating a gift trade, or taking part in free local area occasions and activities.

Making a complete Christmas and New Year spending plan can assist you with dealing with your costs and guarantee you have a monetarily calm Christmas season. Here are a few stages you can follow to make a successful budget,determine your complete accessible assets,Begin by checking what is going on out. Work out how much cash you have accessible to spend on Christmas and New Year costs.

Think about your pay, reserve funds, and any additional assets you can allocate.Distinguish every one of the costs you anticipate during the Christmas season.

This might incorporate gifts, designs, travel costs, food, amusement, and some other exercises or occasions you have arranged. Make certain to consider any extra costs well defined for your practices or family customs. Relegating a particular dollar adds up to each expense class. This will assist you with focusing on your spending and pursue informed decisions. Be practical and obliging of your monetary circumstance while setting these limits.

Research costs and arrangements, Prior to making any buys, research costs to guarantee you are getting the best incentive for your cash. Search for limits, deals, and exceptional advancements that can assist you with saving money on gifts or different things on your list.

As you make buys, record each cost to monitor your spending. Utilize a planning application, bookkeeping sheet, or just a pen and paper to screen your costs and remain inside your designated amounts.

In the event that you end up surpassing your financial plan in any class, consider elective choices to set aside cash. For instance, you could decide on hand crafted gifts or, Prioritize and change on a case by case basis. On the off chance that you observe that your spending plan is getting tight, reconsider your needs and consider changing your spending in specific regions.

Center around what is generally critical to you and your friends and family during the occasion season. When the Christmas season is finished, audit your spending plan and assess how well you adhered to it. Observe any victories or difficulties you confronted and utilize this data to refine your planning abilities for future celebrations.

Making a spending plan is only the initial step. It is fundamental for adhere to your spending plan and oppose the compulsion to overspend. By preparing and being aware of your costs, you can partake in a happy and monetarily mindful Christmas season.

Allocating Funds For Gifts Decorations And Festivities

While distributing assets for gifts, designs, and merriments, it's critical to have a financial plan set up to guarantee that you spend inside your means. Here are a moves toward assist you with dispensing reserves effectively

1•Determine Your General Financial Plan
Begin by concluding the amount you are willing or ready to spend on gifts, beautifications, and celebrations. Consider what is happening and different responsibilities to lay out a practical amount.

2•Prioritize Your Costs
Make a rundown of the multitude of essential costs, like gifts for family and dear companions, improvements for your home or setting, and any arranged celebrations or occasions. Rank these costs in view of their significance to you and the occasion.

3•Set Spending Limits

Set out a particular measure of cash to each expense classification. For gifts, conclude the amount you can spend per individual or lay out a general financial plan for all gifts. With regards to improvements and celebrations, decide the amount you can dispense for every thing or activity.

4•Research And Think About Costs

Set aside some margin to explore costs and analyze choices prior to making any buys. Search for arrangements, limits, or elective choices that fit reasonably affordable for you. This will assist you with pursuing informed choices and possibly save some money.

5•Track Your Spending

Track your costs as you make buys. This will assist you with remaining focused and abstain from overspending. It's vital to consistently survey your spending plan to guarantee that you are allotting reserves wisely.

6•Be Imaginative And Ingenious

Consider Do-It-Yourself improvements or carefully assembled gifts, which can be more practical and customized. Search free of charge or minimal expense happy exercises locally, for example, nearby motorcades or occasion concerts.

7•Be Adaptable

Recollect that surprising costs might emerge, so it's essential to be adaptable with your financial plan. In the event that important, change your spending in one class to oblige changes in another.

Remember, the soul of the time still up in the air by how much cash you spend. It's the idea and exertion behind the gifts and the delight imparted to friends and family that genuinely matter.

Dispensing assets for gifts, enrichments, and celebrations requires cautious preparation and thought.

Here are a few hints to assist you with capitalizing on your budget:

Set A Financial Plan

Decide the amount you can bear to spend on gifts, beautifications, and merriments. Think about your in general financial circumstance and focus on your expenses.

Make A Gift List

Make a rundown of individuals you need to purchase presents for and designate a particular sum for every individual. This will assist you with remaining coordinated and guarantee you don't overspend.

Research Costs And Think About Bargains

Prior to making any buys, research costs and analyze bargains from various stores or online stages. Search for limits, coupons, or extraordinary advancements that can assist you with saving money.

Consider Custom Made Or Customized Gifts

High quality or customized gifts can be a smart and practical choice. Think about your abilities and gifts, and contemplate making something one of a kind for your cherished ones.

Plan Ahead For Beautifications

If conceivable, plan your improvements well ahead of time. This will give you an opportunity to look at the best costs and make the most of any deals or limits. Consider reusing designs from earlier years or acquiring them from companions and family.

Prioritize Encounters Over Material Things

Rather than zeroing in exclusively on material gifts, consider giving encounters like passes to a show, a spa day, or an end of the week escape. These encounters can make enduring recollections without overwhelming your budget.

Plan Potluck Or Cost-sharing Occasions

On the off chance that you're facilitating a merry get-together, consider sorting out a potluck or cost-sharing occasion.

Along these lines, everybody can contribute by getting a dish or chipping for costs, making it more reasonable for everybody involved.

Keep Track Of Your Spending

All through the Christmas season, monitor your spending to guarantee you're adhering to your financial plan. Use planning applications or basic accounting sheets to screen your costs and make changes if necessary.

The main thing is the soul of the Christmas season, not how much cash you spend. Center around significant motions, investing energy with friends and family, and making an euphoric air.

CHAPTER FIVE

Investing And Saving For A Bright Financial Future

Effective money management and saving are urgent parts of building a brilliant Financial future. Here are a few nitty gritty bits of knowledge on the most proficient method to move toward both:

Importance of Saving:
Setting aside cash is the underpinning of monetary strength. It gives a security net to crises and assists you with accomplishing your objectives. Here are a few central issues to consider:

A• Planning:
Make a financial arrangement to follow your pay and compensation. Designate a piece of your pay to reserve funds each month.

B•Put forth Reserve funds Objectives

Characterize present moment and long haul objectives, like putting something aside for an initial installment, a get-away, or retirement. Having explicit objectives assists you with remaining motivated.

C•Secret Stash

Put away three to a half year of everyday costs in an effectively open bank account. This asset goes about as a pad during startling occasions like employment cutback or clinical emergencies.

D•Robotize Reserve Funds

Set up programmed moves from your financial records to a bank account to guarantee reliable investment funds without manual effort.

E•Understanding Contributing

Putting away permits your cash to develop over the long run. It includes placing your capital into different resources with the assumption for acquiring returns. This is the very thing that you really want to know.

A•Instruct Yourself

Gain proficiency with the nuts and bolts of effective money management, including different resource classes like stocks, securities, land, and common assets. Comprehend the dangers related with every venture option.

B•Characterize Your Gamble Resistance

Evaluate your gamble resilience in view of variables like your age, financial objectives, and individual solace level. This decides the fitting venture strategy.

C•Broadening: Spread your ventures across various resource classes and inside every resource class. Enhancement mitigates gambles and expands potential returns.

D•Venture Records

Consider charging advantaged accounts like Individual Retirement Records (IRAs) or 401(k) plans for long haul retirement investment funds. Exploit any business matching contributions.

E• Look for Proficient Counsel

In the event that you're uncertain or miss the mark on opportunity to deal with your speculations, counsel a monetary consultant who can give direction in light of your objectives and chance tolerance.

F•Screen and Rebalance

Routinely audit your venture portfolio to guarantee it lines up with your objectives. Make changes if important to keep up with enhancement and adjust to changing business sector conditions.

G•Time and Accumulate Interest

One of the most impressive parts of effective financial planning is the idea of accumulating funds. It permits your speculations to develop dramatically by reinvesting the income. The previous you begin money management, the more noteworthy the advantages of compounding.

Opportunities For Season Investments

1. Retail And Buyer Merchandise Organizations
With the Christmas season being a rush hour for shopping, putting resources into retail and shopper products organizations can be a rewarding an open door.

2. Travel And The Tourism Industry
As individuals frequently travel during the Christmas season, putting resources into the movement and the travel industry can be a productive choice.

3. Innovation Organizations
With the rising pattern of web based shopping and computerized giving, putting resources into innovation organizations that take special care of seasonal shopping and giving can be a brilliant move.

4. Amusement And Recreation Industry

With individuals searching for no particular reason and bubbly exercises during the Christmas season, putting resources into diversion and relaxation organizations can introduce open doors for development.

5. Food And Drink Organizations

As individuals enjoy merry devouring and feasting out during special times of year, putting resources into food and refreshment organizations can be a promising choice.

Occasional speculations can give various open doors to financial backers to benefit from explicit market patterns and occasional changes.

For instance, putting resources into the travel industry throughout the late spring months or in retail organizations during the Christmas season can yield huge returns. Furthermore, horticultural ventures can profit from occasional changes in climate and harvest yields.

In Conclusion,understanding and making the most of these occasional open doors can be a worthwhile technique for financial backers hoping to broaden their portfolios and expand their profits.

Long Term Saving Strategies For Christmas Expenses

Long term saving Strategies for Christmas and New Year costs include arranging and planning great ahead of time to guarantee that you have an adequate number of assets to cover all of your vacation costs. Here are a few hints to assist you with putting something aside for the Christmas season:

1. Begin Early

Start saving cash for Christmas and New Year costs as soon as could really be expected. By beginning to save a while ahead of time, you can fan out the financial weight and keep away from the pressure of attempting to concoct an enormous amount of cash at the same time.

2. Make A Financial Plan

Decide the amount you intend to spend on gifts, enrichments, travel, and other occasion related costs. When you have an unmistakable thought of your expected expenses, you can dispense a particular measure of cash every month to put towards your vacation reserve.

3. Set Up A Different Investment Account

Consider opening a committed bank account explicitly for your Christmas and New Year costs. This can assist you with monitoring your advancement and keep you from plunging into these assets for different purposes.

4. Scale Back Trivial Costs

Search for ways of diminishing your optional spending to let loose more cash for your vacation investment funds. This could include scaling back feasting out, diversion, or other trivial buys.

5. Think About Elective Kinds Of Revenue

In the event that you're battling to find additional cash in your spending plan, ponder taking on a seasonal work, selling things you never again need, or tracking down alternate ways of producing extra pay explicitly reserved for occasion costs.

6. Exploit Discounts And Deals

Over time, watch out for deals and discounts on things that you intend to buy for these special seasons. By making the most of these open doors, you can extend your vacation financial plan further.

7. Do-It-Yourself Gifts And Adornments

Consider making natively constructed gifts or enhancements to get a good deal on vacation costs. Not exclusively can this be a fun and inventive cash saving tip, yet it can likewise add an individual touch to your vacation festivities.

8. Use Cash-back And Rewards Programs

Exploit cash-back and rewards programs presented by Mastercards or shopping applications to bring in additional cash or limits on your vacation buys. This can assist with extending your financial plan further and set aside you cash over the long haul.

9. Shop Slow Time Of Year

Consider buying occasion related things during off-busy times, like after Christmas or during deals consistently. This can assist you with getting a good deal on improvements, wrapping paper, and other occasion fundamentals.

10. Plan Reasonable Exercises
Rather than costly excursions or occasions, search for reasonable or free exercises to appreciate during the Christmas season. This can assist you with getting a good deal on diversion while as yet making paramount encounters with your friends and family.

11. Speak With Loved Ones
Have transparent discussions with your loved ones about your vacation spending plan. Defining assumptions and limits can assist with reducing monetary strain and guarantee that everybody is in total agreement with regards to gift-giving and festivities.

By carrying out these drawn out saving systems, you can assume command over your vacation expenses and keep away from the pressure of overspending during the Christmas and New Year season. With cautious preparation and planning, you can partake in special times of year without forfeiting your financial prosperity.

By following these drawn out saving systems, you can guarantee that you have the monetary assets expected to cover your Christmas and New Year costs without venturing into the red or feeling overpowered by the financial type of the Christmas season.

Preparing and being focused about saving can assist you with partaking in special times of year without agonizing over the effect on your funds.

CHAPTER SIX

Practical Tips For Practicing Financial Discipline During Christmas

1. Set A Financial Plan

Before the Christmas season starts, make a spending plan that frames the amount you can bear to spend on presents, designs, and different costs. Adhere to this spending plan to try not to overspend and amassing obligation.

2. Begin Saving Early

Start saving cash for occasion costs over time. This can assist with mitigating the financial weight of the Christmas season and forestall the need to depend on Visas or credits to take care of expenses.

3. Focus On Your Spending

Figure out which occasion costs are generally essential to you and apportion your financial plan in like manner. Center around what gives you and your friends and family the most pleasure and think about scaling back superfluous buys.

4. Examination Shop

Get some margin to think about costs and search for bargains prior to making any buys. This can assist you with tracking down the best incentive for your cash and try not to overspend on things that might be accessible at a lower cost somewhere else.

5. Keep Away From Drive Purchasing

Fight the temptation to make motivation buys, particularly during deals or special occasions. Adhere to your financial plan and just purchase things that you have anticipated ahead of time.

6. Gifts And Enrichments

Consider making custom made gifts or designs to get a good deal on vacation costs. Not exclusively can this be a tomfoolery and imaginative cash saving tip, yet it add an individual touch to your vacation festivities.

7. Use Cash-back And Rewards Programs

Exploit cash-back and rewards programs presented by Visas or shopping applications to bring in additional cash or limits on your vacation buys. This can assist with extending your spending plan further and set aside you cash over the long haul.

8. Shop Slow Time Of Year

Consider buying occasion related things during off-busy times, like after Christmas or during deals consistently. This can assist you with getting a good deal on improvements, wrapping paper, and other occasion basics.

9. Plan Reasonable Exercises

Rather than costly excursions or occasions, search for reasonable or free exercises to appreciate during the Christmas season.

This can assist you with getting a good deal on diversion while as yet making critical encounters with your friends and family.

10. Speak With Loved Ones

Have transparent discussions with your loved ones about your vacation financial plan.

Defining assumptions and limits can assist with reducing monetary strain and guarantee that everybody is in total agreement with regards to gift-giving and festivities.

11. Use Coupons And Rebate Codes

Search for coupons and markdown codes to utilize while making occasion buys. Numerous retailers offer extraordinary advancements during the Christmas season, so make the most of these investment funds potential open doors.

12. Consider A Present Trade

Rather than purchasing individual presents for each relative or companion, consider coordinating a present trade where every individual just gets one gift for another member. This can assist with decreasing the general expense of gift-giving.

13. Shop At Secondhand Shops Or Transfer Shops

Investigate secondhand shops and transfer looks for interesting and reasonable occasion gifts and designs. You wouldn't believe the fortunes you can find for a portion of the expense of new things.

14. Limit Travel Costs

In the event that you ordinarily travel during special times of year, search for ways of limiting your movement costs. Consider carpooling, utilizing public transportation, or tracking down limited airfare and facilities to get a good deal on movement costs.

15. Have A Potluck Or BYOB Gathering

On the off chance that you're facilitating an occasion gathering, think about requesting that visitors contribute a dish or bring their own refreshments. This can assist with dispersing the expense of food and beverages and make the occasion more reasonable for everybody.

16. Give The Endowment Of Encounters

Rather than actual gifts, consider giving the endowment of encounters, for example, show passes, gallery participations, or spa days. These gifts can make enduring recollections without adding to material belongings.

17. Exploit Free Transportation

While shopping on the web, search for retailers that proposition free delivery on vacation buys. This can assist you with getting a good deal on conveyance charges and keep away from the need to make extra in-store trips.

18. Plan For Post-holiday Sales:

If conceivable, hold on until after the Christmas season to make specific buys. Numerous retailers offer critical limits on vacation things once the season has passed, permitting you to load up for the next year at a lower cost.

19. Keep Away From Pointless Costs Assess your vacation customs and consider whether there are any superfluous costs that can be wiped out. For instance, on the off chance that you regularly convey elaborate occasion cards, consider deciding on a more practical other option.

20. Monitor Your Spending

Monitor your vacation costs all through the season to guarantee that you're remaining acceptable for you. This can assist you with distinguishing any regions where you might be overspending and make changes on a case by case basis.

Carrying out these drawn out saving systems, you can assume command over your vacation expenses and stay away from the pressure of overspending during the Christmas and New Year season.

With cautious preparation and planning, you can partake in special times of year without forfeiting your monetary prosperity.

Avoiding Impulsive Spending And Overspending

Avoiding Impulsive Spending And Overspending

One of the greatest difficulties during the Christmas season is staying away from indiscreet spending and overspending.

With the strain to purchase presents, beautify, and engage, it's not difficult to become involved with the fervor and spend beyond what you can bear.

Here are a few techniques to assist you with staying away from indiscreet spending and overspending during special times of year:

1. Set A Financial Plan

Before you start your vacation shopping, find opportunity to make a spending plan for gifts, designs, food, and different costs. Be reasonable about what you can stand to spend and adhere to your financial plan however much as could be expected.

2. Make A Rundown

Make a rundown of the multitude of individuals you really want to purchase presents for and the things you need to buy. Having a reasonable arrangement can assist you with trying not to make drive buys and keep fixed on what you really need.

3. Abstain From Shopping When Pushed

It's not difficult to make drive buys while you're feeling anxious or overpowered. Attempt to abstain from shopping while you're feeling personal, as this can prompt overspending.

4. Use Cash

Consider utilizing cash rather than Mastercards for your vacation buys. At the point when you have a restricted measure of money to spend, it's simpler to adhere to your financial plan and abstain from overspending.

5. Stand By Prior To Making A Buy

If you find something you need to purchase, take a stab at holding up 24 hours prior to making the buy. This can assist you with deciding whether it's something you truly need or on the other hand on the off chance that it's simply an off the cuff hasty purchase.

6. Keep Away From Deals Pressure: Retailers frequently use deals strategies to pressure customers into making buys. Be aware of these strategies and fight the temptation to purchase something since it's marked down.

7. Shop With A Companion
Consider shopping with a companion who can assist with keeping you responsible and give a second assessment on likely buys. Having another person there can assist you with trying not to pursue indiscreet choices.

8. Focus On Encounters Over Material Gifts

Rather than burning through cash on costly gifts, consider giving the endowment of encounters, for example, a custom made dinner, a roadtrip, or a pleasant movement. These can be more significant and paramount than material belongings.

9. Do-It-Yourself Gifts And Adornments
Get innovative and make your own presents and beautifications as opposed to getting them. Not exclusively will this set aside you cash, yet it can add an individual touch to your vacation festivities.

10. Set Practical Assumptions
Converse with your loved ones about setting sensible assumptions for gift-giving. Consider doing a gift trade or drawing a spending line for diminish the financial tension for all interested parties.

11. Exploit Deals And Limits
Assuming that you in all actuality do have to make buys, search for deals, limits, and coupons to assist

with extending your spending plan further. Simply make certain to adhere to your rundown and keep away from superfluous buys.

12. Prepare For Occasion Feasts And Gatherings

Rather than overspending on food and beverages for occasion social affairs, prepare and shop decisively to set aside cash. Consider potluck-style dinners to impart the expense for other people.

13. Practice Appreciation

Recall that the Christmas season is tied in with investing energy with friends and family and showing appreciation, not about material belongings. Center around the things that genuinely matter and relinquished the strain to overspend.

14. Screen Your Spending

Monitor your vacation costs and consistently audit your financial plan to guarantee you're remaining focused. This can assist you with recognizing any regions where you might be overspending and make changes on a case by case basis.

15. Begin Saving Right On Time For The Following Year

To keep away from monetary pressure during future special seasons, begin saving cash right off the bat in the year explicitly for occasion costs. This can assist with lightening the strain to overspend when special times of year roll around once more.

By following these procedures, you can decrease the gamble of hasty spending and overspending during the Christmas season, permitting you to partake in the merriments without the pressure of financial strain.

Making Smart Choices For Affordable Gifts And Celebrations

Secret Santa

Rather than purchasing presents for each relative or companion, consider coordinating a Secret Santa present trade where every individual just needs to get one gift inside a set spending plan.

Home Made Designs

Rather than purchasing costly occasion enrichments, consider causing your own utilizing materials you as of now to have at home. This can be a fun and spending plan well disposed method for adding an individual touch to your vacation style.

Regift Things

In the event that you have unused or previously owned things that you got as gifts and don't need, consider regifting them to somebody who might see the value in them. Simply make a point to do so insightfully and keep away from regifting to the first provider.

Shop At Secondhand Shops Or Transfer Shops
You can find remarkable and reasonable gifts at secondhand shops or transfer shops. This is an incredible cash saving tip and backing maintainable shopping rehearsals.

Plan A Gift Trade Game
Rather than customary gift-giving, plan a tomfoolery gift trade game like Trinket or Yankee Trade. This adds a component of energy and guarantees that everybody gets a gift without burning through a truckload of cash.

Utilize Free Or Minimal Expense Occasion Exercises
Search for nothing or minimal expense occasion exercises in your space, like light shows, local area occasions, or open air ice skating. This permits you to partake in the Christmas season without burning through huge amounts of cash.

Give The Endowment Of Time

Propose to assist a companion or relative with undertakings or tasks, or invest quality energy with them accomplishing something they appreciate. Once in a while the most significant gifts are those that cost nothing by any means.

Potluck Social Occasions

In the event that you're facilitating a special festival, consider requesting that visitors carry a dish to share. This not just decreases the expense for you as the host, however it additionally permits everybody to add to the feast.

Set A Financial Plan

Before you begin looking for gifts or arranging occasions, set a practical spending plan and stick to it. This will assist you with trying not to overspend and hold your funds in line.

Search For Arrangements And Limits

Watch out for deals, limits, and advancements while looking for gifts or occasion basics. You can likewise think about utilizing coupons or cashback applications to get a good deal on your buys.

Focus On Encounters Over Material Presents
Rather than purchasing actual things, think about giving the endowment of encounters like passes to a show, a spa day, or a cooking class. These encounters make enduring recollections without burning through every last dollar.

Settling on brilliant decisions for reasonable gifts and festivities, you can partake in the Christmas season without overwhelming your funds. Everything revolves around being aware of your spending and tracking down innovative ways of commending without overspending.

Strategies For Resisting Social Pressure And Keeping A Healthy Financial Mindset

1. Adhere To Your Financial Plan

Set a practical spending plan for your vacation spending and stick to it, paying little mind to prevalent burden to overspend. Advise yourself that remaining inside your method is a higher priority than attempting to stay aware of others.

2. Be Straightforward With Others

Assuming that you're feeling forced to spend beyond what you can manage, be transparent with your loved ones about your financial circumstance. A great many people will comprehend and value your trustworthiness.

3. Center Around Encounters, Not Material Belongings

Advise yourself that the Christmas season is tied in with making recollections and investing energy with friends and family, not tied in with purchasing the most recent contraptions or costly presents. Focus on encounters over material belongings to oppose prevailing difficulty to overspend.

4. Encircle Yourself With Similar People
Invest energy with loved ones who share your qualities and financial attitude. This can assist with lessening the prevalent difficulty to overspend and establish a steady climate for adhering to your spending plan.

5. Practice Self Care
Deal with your psychological and profound prosperity by defining limits and focusing on your own financial wellbeing. Recollect that it's alright to express no to get-togethers or gift trades that don't line up with your spending plan and values.

6. Look For Help From Others
On the off chance that you're battling to oppose prevailing difficulty to overspend, look for help from a confided in companion, relative, or monetary counselor. Discussing your interests and getting

counsel from others can assist you with keeping focused with your monetary objectives.

CHAPTER SEVEN

Embracing Financial Planning For A Merry And Debt Free Christmas And New Year Season

Embracing financial expectations of a cheerful and commitment-free Christmas and New Year remembers making due with mindful decisions about how to spend and save cash during the Christmas season.

The following are a positive maneuvers toward help with achieving this goal:

Plan a present trade game: Rather than purchasing individual presents for everybody, plan a tomfoolery present trade game like Trinket or Yankee Trade. This guarantees that everybody gets a gift without burning through huge load of cash

Remain dynamic:

Coordinate real work into your ordinary practice to diminish strain and lift your disposition. Whether it's going for a stroll, practicing yoga, or taking part in a colder season sport, staying dynamic can help you with regulating strain during the event season.

Associate with loved ones:

Track down an open door to connect with your loved ones and spotlight on quality time together. Whether it's straightening out a family game night or working with a virtual social gathering, empowering critical affiliations can give delight and reduce strain during the event season.

Plan standard seasons of rest and loosening up all through the Christmas season. Whether it's a quiet night at home or a week's end escape, attempt to recharge and appreciate respites from the clamoring celebrations.

Review that exceptional seasons needn't bother with being perfect. License yourself to surrender outlandish presumptions and embrace the imperfections that go with the season. Based on making huge memories as opposed to having a go at flawlessness.

Work On Utilizing Time Gainfully:

Make a schedule or plan for the day to truly help with managing your time. Center around tasks, set sensible deadlines, and avoid overcommitting yourself to avoid pointless pressure.

These goals can be custom fitted to your own tendencies and conditions. Pick the ones that influence you and change them to make a peaceful Christmas and New Year season that suits your necessities.

Embracing monetary making arrangements for a joyful and obligation free Christmas and New Year includes coming to cognizant conclusions about how to spend and set aside cash during the Christmas season.

By embracing monetary preparation and coming to cognizant conclusions about how to spend and set aside cash during the Christmas season, you can have a joyful and obligation free Christmas and New Year. Everything revolves around being aware of your funds and tracking down innovative ways of commending without overspending.

By executing these means, you can assume command over your funds during the Christmas and New year season and partake in an obligatory free and blissful festival with your friends and family.

Everything revolves around being purposeful with your spending and tracking down significant ways of praising without monetary pressure.

Reflection On The Benefits Of A Well Planned Christmas And New Year Season

Consider the advantages of a very much arranged Christmas and New Year season.

The bubbly time frame, which incorporates both Christmas and New Year, is a period of delight, festivity and reflection for some individuals all over the planet.

The festivals can at times appear to be overpowering because of the large number of errands and obligations, a very much arranged Christmas and New Year occasion offers many advantages past the quick delight of the festivals. Here are a few considerations on the advantages of an efficient get-away:

Less Pressure

By preparing, you can limit the pressure of last-minute arrangements. A thoroughly examined timetable and agenda will assist you with remaining coordinated, delegate undertakings, and guarantee everything is done on time.

This will diminish the gamble of feeling overpowered and permit you to partake in the season to the fullest.

Time With Your Friends And Family
The Christmas season offers the ideal chance to invest energy with loved ones. By preparing, you can arrange plans, sort out gatherings, and make significant minutes. Whether you're facilitating a Christmas supper, going to a party, or essentially going through a comfortable night at home with friends and family, a very much arranged season guarantees you have sufficient opportunity and energy to interface with those you care about most will be generally significant.

Greater Inventiveness
An efficient excursion period permits you to release your innovativeness. From enriching your home to arranging occasion exercises, you can investigate your imaginative side and make your festivals extra special.

Meaningful Customs

A very much arranged Christmas season gives a valuable chance to keep up with and make significant practices. Whether it's baking treats, watching exemplary motion pictures, chipping in for a nearby cause, or going to faith gatherings, customs assume a significant part in making this season unique.

Through preparing, you can guarantee that these customs are remembered for your timetable and celebrated by all interested parties. Taking care of oneself and health: The Christmas season ought to be a period of bliss and unwinding, however it can be a period of physical and close to home fatigue. All around arranged Christmas and New Year occasions generally lead to great festivals.